You Can't Fool God

Soul Searching Poetry

by

Jacqueline Johnson

authorHOUSE®

AuthorHouse™
1663 Liberty Drive, Suite 200
Bloomington, IN 47403
www.authorhouse.com
Phone: 1-800-839-8640

First published by AuthorHouse 9/13/2007

ISBN: 978-1-4343-2882-3 (sc)

Printed in the United States of America
Bloomington, Indiana

This book is printed on acid-free paper.

Dedication

This book is dedicated to my husband, Lonnie Johnson, of 21 years,

And

Cole Hill Christian Methodist Episcopal Church Family

For

Their support and prayers,

To God be the Glory!

Introduction

Thanks be unto God for getting me to this point in my life. On so many occasions, I heard His voice, but chose to listen to that of a stranger. I had to learn the hard way, that for every choice we make, there is a consequence. For everything, there is season. There are so many missed opportunities because the task seems too hard from our fleshly vision. We lean on our own understanding, which is very limited. So many times when we're facing oppositions or challenges in our lives, we become discouraged or even depressed. We discover later that it was a strength and faith builder to help us get to our destination. If we're given a position we're not prepared for, we are easily broken. Our oppositions are merely opportunities for spiritual growth. God's will for us is to be happy and prosperous. I believe inside all of His children, there lies a hidden treasure. As you grow spiritually and begin to seek God and pray, in due time, your treasure will be revealed and manifested for God's glorification. In my own life experiences, I found it hard to step out of my comfort zone. As long as I could somewhat figure things out in my own mind, I felt confident. As God continually put me on the potter's wheel, I began to walk more by faith and not by sight. I am truly a witness that when you're obedient to the will of God, He will take you to levels in your life that you never, ever, imagined. Whatever the journey might be, God will equip you for it.

At an early age, as I faced difficult situations, God always gave me words to write to get me through them. These words always gave comfort to my hurting heart. I never realized that He was shaping and molding me for such a time as this. Oh, what an awesome God we serve. It's as if I was a priceless piece of china sitting in the cabinet only to be looked upon. I must be honest, for a while, I was satisfied with just sitting there looking pretty. Then one day, I noticed the dust was beginning to cover me and I started to feel I had no purpose anymore. No one could look at me and see the beautiful designs or the reflection of what I truly represented. The real me was hidden. It's like trying to look at yourself through a dirty mirror. To see true results, the mirror must be cleaned. Although, man was looking at the outside, God seen my heart. He came along and breathed on me,

cleansing me to be a witness for the world. I'm so glad that God keeps His collector's items clean.

As you read, I pray that these poems will compel you to take a look in the mirror. We often want to hear words that make us feel good about ourselves; but only the truth will set us free. If we're guilty, we're guilty. It's time for the children of God to take a stand for righteousness.

I prayed with a sincere heart for God to give me words to say during a storm in my life on April 2, 2002. He gave me the poem, From the Pulpit To The Pews, on April 3, 2002. He is still investing in me. Often times, I found myself being convicted. I discovered, I had no room to talk about anyone. Take a self- evaluation, and to yourself be true. Remember, YOU CAN'T FOOL GOD!

Contents

Family Poetry

Short Story Poetry

Dedications

The Dream I Dreamed
(True Testimony)

It had been a beautiful day, but now it was night
I can't remember if I said my prayers or not,
Although I was taught that was right
I crawled into bed; I don't remember what was on my mind
But when I fell asleep, God had a message for me at that time
I was at my mom's house as I stood and looked outside
The wind began to blow uncontrollably, and the clouds opened wide
It suddenly became very dark as the clouds rolled toward the earth
I began to pray, for all it was worth
I was crying and telling God that I wasn't ready yet
It was a dream I'll never forget
Out of the kitchen, my Mom came running, already realizing what was going on
Calling out, "Jehovah God, I'm ready, I'm ready to go home!"
I'll never forget this as long as I live
God showed me that He's coming back for real
He also showed me that if he came back that particular night
Where I would spend eternity
I thank God for the vision, for letting me see
I woke up crying out of control, as I looked out the window to see if the dream was really real
Afterwards, thanking God for giving me another chance,
And for all my sins, I knew that He would forgive
My husband woke up trying to calm me down, telling me I was just dreaming
But I knew deep in my heart, this particular dream had a true meaning
For some time, I cried and wiped many tears,
But to God be the glory, for getting me on the right path over the years!

From The Pulpit To The Pews

Are you proclaiming to be a child of God on Sunday?
And full of lies, deceit, envy, and jealousy on Monday?
Are you one that says, I can tell you things in confidentiality
But just cant wait until I leave?
Spreading my business, telling whatever and whomever you please?
From the sincerity of your heart, do you help me when I'm in need
Or is it only to be recognized for doing a good deed?
When I'm down and out and I need an encouraging word from you,
Do you talk about me behind my back and say things that are untrue?
Is it always what you say goes, and you don't have to listen to anyone
else?
Do you block the opinion of others out, and only listen to yourself?
Are you always right and everyone else is wrong?
Are you always lifting yourself up, and not giving praises to whom
they belong?
Do you honestly seek spiritual guidance in all that you do
Or have you placed yourself upon a pedestal, and think the world
revolves around you?
Has God blessed you with a heavenly voice to sing?
Do you use it to glorify His name, or for saying mean and devilish
things?
Has God blessed you with musical hands to play?
Do you use it to your advantage, to satisfy your own selfish ways?
Has God chosen you to go out and teach?
Are you spreading the good news, or gossip to those you meet?
If I lost my home and had no place for me or my children to lay our
heads,
Would you open your doors to keep us warm, and make sure my
children were fed?
Most importantly, if I came to you for spiritual guidance, and asked
you to pray,
Would you know how to open the prayer line to God, and know what
to say?
Is He truly the head of your house
Or is He second in line, coming after you, your lover, or spouse?
If we truly put God first in all that we say and do,
We would be on one accord, starting from the PULPIT TO THE
PEWS!

What Really Matters

It's not about the color of your skin
What really matters is what's deep within
It doesn't matter if you're black or white, red or blue
But instead, having the love of Christ inside of you
It's not about the length of your hair, nor your shape or size
But living a life that's pleasing in God's eyes
It's not about the size of your house, or fancy automobile
It's about walking in faith, and doing God's will
It's not important where you work, or what position you hold on
your job
But giving of your earnings what is owed, and not robbing God
What's important is the way you carry yourself, not the way you
dress
It's not whether you win or lose, but doing your best
It's not about who was right or wrong, but being able to forgive
It's not how much money you make, but how you live
It's not about having a bachelor or master's degree
What really matters is how you treat me
It's not about just going to church on Sunday morning to hear
The word, but spreading God's message outside the church walls
It's knowing His word for yourself, and going wherever you're
needed or called
It's not about what I hear you say, nor what I see you do
What matters is knowing only God is a righteous judge,
And He's watching you!

Can You Imagine?

Have you ever just stopped and watched the clouds
Letting your imagination run wild, and laughing out loud?
Making something out of everything you see
Whatever you imagine, that's what it seems to be
Have you ever imagined God sitting there on top of a cloud looking down?
His eyes are focused on you, and at first He doesn't make a sound.
He reaches and picks up a book as He begins to stand
You realize its The Book of Life that He holds in His hand
Out loud He begins to read
He calls out your name and says, "I am well pleased."
You can now see His face and there's a big smile
He tells you, you are worthy to be called His child
He says you ran a good race and you were faithful over a few things
So for you, God has a pair of angelic wings
You're crying and there's absolutely nothing you can say
Then God reaches for your hand, and together you fly away!

God's Spiritual Makeover

When you find yourself looking in the mirror, just what is it that you see?
Is it someone beautiful on the inside with their own identity?
Or is it someone wondering, what do others think of me?
Trying to live up to man's definition of beautiful can drive you insane
With God as your beauty consultant, true beauty can be obtained
You must realize, man will lift you up one minute and tear you down the next
Without God's spiritual makeover, in your mind,
The tongue can leave a lasting negative effect
You will find yourself in the late midnight hour crying as you lay in your bed
Feeling lonely, hopeless, and depressed, because of what someone said
You'll then discover that none of your materialistic possessions
Can give you peace of mind
I recommend that you try God's spiritual makeover at this time
Why not invest in God's beauty parlor, by reading and
Meditating on His word, getting a makeover that's complete
You'll have a new walk, a new talk, a changed person from your head to your feet
There will be a glow about you that will make heads turn, stop, and stare
When God gets through with you, there's just something special and awesome there
You won't have to wear a sign to advertise because people will see the change
And come to you
 Saying, "there's something different, just what did you do?"
This is an opportunity for you to share the beauty tips,
Not secrets, of God's spiritual transformation
Not going on hearsay, but an on hand education
It doesn't matter how many times you hear, "You're beautiful,"
Coming from someone else
You've got to feel it from deep within, and know it for yourself.

Temporary Solutions

So you think you can solve all your problems by getting drunk off of your beer?
While under the influence, what if you hurt someone you love so dear?
Causing your pain after the hangover, to be even more severe
There is a problem solver who can give you a lasting cure!
You say you can deal with your problems after you've had that smoke.
Tell me, when the thrill is gone, how will you cope?
There is someone who can still give you hope!
You say you feel better when you go shopping for yourself,
Having some quality time
Not caring that the bills are due, and falling farther behind
Why settle for temporary satisfaction,
When there is someone who can bring peace to your troubled mind?
Go ahead and eat up everything, it makes you feel better, so it seems
Next you'll be overweight and develop an even lower self-esteem
There is someone who can make everything about you, new and clean!
There is a lasting solution to your problems, and to you there is no cost
His name is Jesus, and free of charge, He died on the cross
He requires that you take up your cross and follow Him
He'll be your light in darkness, so your path won't remain dim
He'll set you free, and in life, He'll be all that you need
Because whom the Son of God sets free, is free indeed!

Whom Will You Serve?

In your life, there will be some very important decisions to make
One being; choosing to follow God or the devil;
Which path will you take?
You can't serve two masters at one time
It's one or the other make up your mind
You can be either hot or cold, lukewarm just won't do
The decision is yours to make, it's up to you
If it's God that you choose
Eternal life is yours, you can't lose
If you choose the devil, your soul will be lost
Making hell your home, is it worth the cost?
You need to make up your mind, for time is at hand
It's either God or the devil, for whom will you stand?

Judging A Book By Its Cover

Don't say that you want to be with me
When it's only my outer beauty that you see
I can be sexy, and really, really fine
But I can also be foolish, and a waste of your time
There are a lot of hidden secrets you might discover
When you judge a book by its cover!

I might turn you on with my smooth talk
Or even give you chills, when you watch me walk
But I can be a black widow spider,
And in my web, I want you caught
There is a lot about me, you just might happen to discover
When you judge a book by its cover!

And if at first sight, to your eyes I don't appeal
When you get to know me on the inside,
It could change the way you feel
You see, that's when my true identity will be revealed
I don't have to be built like an Amazon to give you chills,
Or have a smooth talk, to convince you that my love is real
So, never, ever, judge a book by its cover
You might be surprised by the things you'll eventually discover!

The Time Of Your Departure

Outside the gate is where all your excess baggage must remain
That is, if you are a passenger boarding God's heavenly plane
You will have to undergo a thorough search
If there is anything that shouldn't be, it will set off the security alert
Before boarding, every knee must bow and every tongue must confess
You must leave behind all the worldly goods that you possess
The only luggage allowed is love, charity, hope, and faith
If found guilty of not having these qualities,
You'll never make it pass the gate
Won't it be wonderful to see God's face
As He lifts his arms to tell you come on through?
Saying, "We'll be flying first class my child, I've been waiting for you."

You Will Know A Tree By The Fruit It Bears

How will the world know that you are a follower of Christ?
Is it demonstrated in your everyday life?
Is it God's Fruits of the Spirit that blossoms from your tree,
Or is it the forbidden fruit that causes you not to spiritually see?
You will know a tree by the fruit that it bears
It's what you demonstrate, not what you declare
There are ravening wolves in sheep's clothing lurking around
Seeking whom they may devour and cut down
Eventually, their own mouth will become a testimony against
Them, causing defeat
Out of the heart, the mouth speaks
When you dip a bucket in the well to draw water,
Trash comes up also, if it's in the well
If evil is in your heart, your mouth will also tell
By your own words you will be condemned if you are untrue
Remember, besides God, someone else is always watching you
Depending on the fruit your tree bears,
A person can be lead to doubt or believe
Your life may be the only Bible someone reads!

Your Spiritual Anchor

Just picture a boy flying a kite
It goes so high in the sky, it's out of his sight
He knows it's there, because its pull he can feel
Just like we can't see our spiritual anchor,
But we know it's real
Imagine the wind blowing through you hair
You can feel its power, so you know it's there
Imagine being on a ship with the anchor down
You can feel it holding you,
Even with the winds raging all around
Think of the last raging storm you went through
You didn't make it out because of the goodness of you
When going through life's storms,
You surely want an anchor that's going to hold
That's why you should make Jesus the anchor of your soul
You see, there will be storms in our lives
Where we'll be tossed to and fro
His anchor is steadfast, and unmovable, never letting you go
No sailor wants his anchor returning to the ship before it is safe
Having God as your anchor is assurance,
You will endure the race.

Don't Leave Home Without It

You can have Visa, MasterCard, or even an American Express
But never leave home without God's word, it's better than all the rest
With man made cards you can go over your limit,
And they will void your transaction
God's word will never return void, it's 100 percent satisfaction
No matter what your previous credit history says,
You won't be denied or turned down
It will put you back on the right track and turn your life around
You can use it in the uttermost parts of the world
It doesn't discriminate against any man, woman, boy or girl
It never charges you interest or a late fee
Use it all day, everyday, and you get the increase
When you read the fine print, you won't find any hidden secrets,
Or anything misleading
You'll receive an added bonus, the minute you start believing
God's word will never leave you stranded, needing assistance from on star
It's able to put you on the right track, no matter where you are
Whether you make your bed in heaven or hell, it will be there too
I wouldn't leave home without it, if I were you!

When You Let God In

God stands at the door and knocks, why don't you let him in?
Your life will never be the same again
Letting God into your heart is definitely worthwhile
He will turn your frowns into smiles
He will turn your complaints into compliments
As well as your struggles into your strengths
Your problems will become your praise
He will even turn your midnights into days
Your depression becomes your determination
Your gossip turns into gospel, you'll have a new conversation
Where you were once blind, you'll be able to see
Your opposition is now an opportunity
Your brokenness becomes your breakthrough
Whatever had you bound, can no longer hold you
Laughter takes the place of your tears
While faith overpowers your fears
When you open the door to our Lord and Savior Jesus Christ
Your barrenness, or emptiness becomes life!

Give Me My Flowers Now

Give me my flowers now
Tomorrow might be too late
Tell me you love me while I'm alive and well
Not on my funeral date.

Give me my flowers now, while I can hear
Don't tell others when I'm dead and gone
Talk to me face to face and be sincere
Don't wait until God calls me home.

Give me my flowers now, while I can see
Stop by sometimes and visit with me
Give me my flowers now
Whether it be roses from the garden,
Or lilies from the field
Give me my flowers now, while I yet live!

God's Got Your Back

I started out with prayer before I started my day
For I knew that the devil would shoot some fiery darts my way
I had to make sure I was fully and properly dressed
Therefore, I started with my loins girt about with truth,
Having on the breastplate of righteousness
My feet were shod with the preparation of the gospel of peace
I walked with assurance; I would keep the devil under my feet
I had to put on the whole armour of God to protect my heart
Therefore, I dressed with the shield of faith, to quench the fiery darts
I proceeded to put on the helmet of salvation, and the sword of the spirit
I had to have the word of God, because demons tremble when they hear it
I was now ready for battle, even if the enemy came from behind and
tried to attack
I was covered from danger seen and unseen, God had my back!

Old Man Death

Sooner or later there will be a knock on your door
Old man death is not far away
This particular knock, you can't run from or ignore
Would you be ready if he came today?

You could be here one minute, and the next you could be gone
That's why you should live in a Christian way
This old world is not our permanent home
Would you be ready if he came today?

Old man death shows up unexpectedly,
No man knows the hour or day
You might not have the opportunity to have last minute words to say
In the twinkling of an eye, your life could be gone
Will you be ready when old man death comes to carry you home?

Stepping On Your Toes

Some people don't like for the truth to be told
By their facial expressions, it sometimes shows
When God is a part of something, the truth will be told
And sometimes that means, stepping on our toes
Your deepest darkest secrets, God already knows
Therefore, your business was already exposed
So there's no need in rolling your eyes, or sneering your nose
Your own path in life, you chose
So if someone told you the truth, and stepped on your toes
Sometimes, that's just the way it goes
Talk to God, confession is good for the soul
Always remember, He is the one in total control!

It's Not About Me

I am the paper and you are the pen
Take the pages of my life Lord, and you fill them in
Write your words on the script of my heart,
And bind them about my neck
Fill me with your Holy Spirit,
So in all thy ways I'll acknowledge you, and never forget
Erase the doubts and fears, and dwell within the uttermost parts of
my soul
Complete me Lord, and make me whole
Use me totally Lord in all thy ways
For you are the potter and I am the clay
Shape and mold me according to thy divine will
So that I may stand boldly to let a dying world know that you live
I am the puppet and you are the strings
Without you Lord, I can't do anything
I'm a lifeless toy only able to function with you as my remote
Without you Lord I'm nothing, there is no hope
So use me for thy divine purpose, so your glory will be revealed
For it's not about me Father, but doing thy Will!

A True Friend

A true friend will settle for less
To ensure that you will get the very best
A true friend will correct you when you are wrong
A true friend will encourage you to do the right thing before you carry on
A true friend will be there, when in your life you make mistakes
A true friend will never give up on you, no matter how long it takes
A true friend will not talk bad about you when you are not around
A true friend will stand up for you when others put you down
A true friend will share with you, their last piece of bread
A true friend will share God's word with you, if you are spiritually dead!

Time Is Running Out

It's sad to say, that after all God has done
It's from His word that you continue to run
People are leaving this world quickly, both old and young
Being caught with their work undone
For some reason, some people feel you have to be old to die
If you read the obituary column, you'll discover that's a lie
Everyday diseases are being diagnosed, and doctors can find no cure
People are not trusting God, and living their lives, full of fear
Time is running out, you might not live to see next year!
You constantly hear about people battling with so many different kinds of cancer
For their quick deterioration, man has no answer
People are having so many heart attacks and strokes
Time is running out, this is no joke!
All of the things God said are being revealed
Time is running out, it's time to do God's will!
Notice how the seasons have changed
In the wintertime, the heat now remains?
People don't fear God anymore, and are constantly using His name in vain
Time is running out, make a change!
Get your life right before it's your name
That the obituary column will obtain!

Preacher Man, Preacher Man

Preacher Man, Preacher Man, are you living like the prodigal son
Trying to please yourself and others, all about having fun?
You're always telling people how to live and what the Bible say
By all means necessary, are you living the right way?
Preacher Man, you of all people should know that you can't
Pull the wool over God's eyes
He can see through any disguise
If you are living like the wolf in sheep clothes
By God's hand, you too will be exposed
In the pulpit preaching God's word, but your sinful life you try to conceal
You can't hide from God Preacher Man, in due time, the truth will be revealed
Can you imagine having to answer to God in the end
When he says, "I have a question for you Preacher Man; Why, Why, Why?
After I sent my only begotten Son on earth for your sins to die?
I tried over and over to get you to turn from your evil ways,
But you ignored my voice, and gave in to the devil day after day
You were appointed the shepherd to keep watch over the flock
They began to stray, because over them, you didn't keep watch
I tried over and over to use you in my ministry and you miserably failed
So depart from me Preacher Man, your home for eternity will be in Hell!"

Making Deals and Broken Promises

Do you find yourself making promises to God, and sometimes you
even make deals?
If He would just get you out of a situation, you'll do His will?
But when He comes through for you, your promise you never fulfill
For him now, you have nothing to give
You can't keep making promises to God, and never change the way you live
The day you went to the doctor for the Pap smear
You were diagnosed with uterus cancer, and this they were sure
You made several promises to God, if He would just make the
cancer disappear
He gave you what you asked, and for the doctors it was an
unexplained cure
Now for God's word, you no longer have a listening ear?
On the same day your baby was conceived
You were diagnosed with having a rare disease
 You cried, begged, and asked God please
For your baby's sake, your sickness, you asked him to relieve
You made several promises as you fell to your knees
For you and the baby, a blessing you received
But now you feel you don't need God in your life to succeed?
The day you had the anxiety attack
You promised God you would give him your life back
When He made you well, in keeping your promises, you were very slack
When it comes to God, you can't keep making promises or deals like that
The situation you were in, you could go right back
If you promise God something, you do just that!

Leave It At The Altar

When you're down and out and in despair
And you go to the altar and pray
Do you leave all of your burdens there?
Or pick them up, as soon as you walk away?

All of your burdens, God can bear
And your help, He won't need
So take it to the altar and leave it there
Then, it's God's word, you must believe!

So whenever you can't seem to find your way
Remember, friends have problems of their own
Go to the altar and sincerely pray
Give it to God, and leave it alone!

Stop Complaining

Do you realize there are millions of children dying of starvation everyday?
And you walk around complaining, with so many negative things to say
Wasting and throwing away food all the time
Not realizing that starving child could be you, never crossed your mind
You have a closet full of clothes, and you're always complaining you have nothing to wear
With a floor full of matching shoes, and you're upset because there is no room to spare
You get up so many mornings, complaining about something as soon as your feet hit the floor,
You come back home some evenings, still nagging as soon as you open the door
EXCUSE ME; but have you ever seen a homeless person living on the street?
Thankful for whatever food he finds to eat?
Digging in nasty trashcans for anything, maybe just something to wear,
Whether it's dirty or clean, he doesn't care
Doing whatever he can to survive,
Struggling from day to day, just to stay alive
So next time you feel you have a reason to complain, just listen to the news
There are people who would love to be in your shoes
So be grateful for what you have, and start each day with a smile
You could be that homeless person, or that starving child!

God's Weather Report

What if the raindrops are actually God's tears?
Can you imagine the amount of crying He's done over the years?
Man has been doing so much cheating, stealing, and lying,
God has to be deeply hurt, what if this is His way of crying?
Before a bad storm, look up at the clouds,
It's as if God is talking to man out loud
When it starts to get dark, He's closing his eyes,
He can no longer watch the devil living in his children's lives
And when the raindrop fall, it is then that he cries
Listen to the thunder; this is God's way of saying that He's upset,
Because for His children, his word has no lasting effect
If the thunder continues to get loud,
He's really fed up with the way man lives, and by no means, is He proud!
You must really be alert if the lightening starts to flash,
He's at the end of his rope, so you better change your ways fast
In your life, he will no longer accept coming last
So next time you look outside, and it's really storming,
From God above, it could be your final warning!

God Works In Mysterious Ways

When you're struggling with something on the inside
That you feel you can only talk to God about
Isn't it strange how things sometimes turn out?
You go to church on Sunday morning to hear an encouraging word
It's like when you talked to God, the pastor also heard
He starts speaking about your situation
And you know from God that this is a confirmation
The text included all that you needed to hear
It's as if the whole time, God was whispering in the pastor's ear
Our prayers are sometimes answered in ways we least expect
So stay alert, you never know who or what God will use next!

Turn It Over To Jesus

Feeling down and out because you lost someone so dear?
I know a friend, that even in the mist of a storm; he can bring about
a ray of cheer!
He's standing there, waiting on you to call out his name,
And when you do, there's a money back guarantee, things will never
be the same
There are a lot of things in life, we will never understand,
But he's our leaning post, always there to lend a helping hand
He sees us when we cry, and I know it's ok,
As long as during the hurt, we allow Him to come in and have His way
Only He can give us that peace, and take away the pain,
So start you healing process, and call on JESUS name!

What Good Does It Do?

What good does it do, to go down on you knees and pray?
When you don't have any faith and believe anyway?
What good does it do to repeatedly ask God to forgive you for your sins?
When you know in your heart, you're going right back to doing the
same old deceitful things again?
What good does it do to say you love the Lord?
When simply speaking to your neighbor is too hard?
What good does it do to give of your offerings and tithes?
When you give it with a grudging heart from the inside?
What good does it do to hold a position in the church?
When you know you won't put forth your best effort and do the work?
When you live a life that is untrue
Just what good does it do?
When you know, from the inside out, God knows you!

Paying Your Tithes

Paying your tithes, you thought you could neglect
Without it having some sort of negative affect?
Trials and tribulations in your life, God will let
So maybe the next time you won't forget
It's very important to always pay your tithes
What comes first in your life, you must decide
Maybe you need to go down on your knees, and in God confide
Because if you spend what is His, you can't hide
And by His word, you must abide.
You can't make it by putting God last
Going out and spending all of your cash
Just shopping everywhere, having a blast
What you have left over, you go home and stash
Then right by the offering plate on Sunday, you bypass
These days you reap what you sow real fast
Before you get home, you might run out of gas
Or who's to say, your car, you might crash
Don't ever think by God's offering table you can dash
Because that money you kept, it won't even last!

What's Love Got To Do With IT? (You Ask)

What's love got to do with it, is the question you dare ask?
Without it, you're headed for a very difficult task
Love must be a part of any relationship if it is going to last
Without love, there is no us, definitely not any trust
Only a temporary condition, built on dishonesty and lust
Love is essential; it is a must
Love is what turns your house into a happy home
It is what keeps the home fire burning strong
Love is like the blood that pumps through your heart
Once it stops flowing, eventually, everything will fall apart
Love is a feeling that should be pure and true when it is spoken
It is not a second, but first class emotion
And with it comes real commitment and devotion
So, if what's love got to do with it, is the question you dare ask?
Well, God is love, and without him, whatever it is, won't last!

Family
Poetry

Good Parents

Good parents communicate with their child before it is born
Doing what the doctor orders, so to their child, they can bring no harm
Usually anxious to know whether it is a boy or girl
But the main focus is that they make it safely into the world
Once it is here, good parents continue to make their child feel safe
By loving and caring for it, every night and day
Sometimes having to stay up all night long with them when
They're sick, keeping their little bottoms clean
Pacing the floors, praying and crying, with no breaks in between
On God, you really learn how to lean
That's what being a good parent means!
For your child, you will learn how to sacrifice
They will become first priority in your life
You put their needs before your own
Good parents start early training at home
Kids learn a lot of things by watching you
Good parents don't say, "Do as I say, and not as I do."
That can be confusing from a child's point of view
Good parents spend quality time with their child each day
Being attentive, and listening to what they have to say
Good parents love their children in spite of their failures in life
Constantly reminding them, no matter what, you can always depend
on Christ!

Making A Difference

If you take a look around, you will realize there are so many vital things that the world lacks
And as each day goes by, another child falls between the cracks
Searching for love and affection he's not getting at home
Trying to find desperately, a place in which he belongs
Morals and values, he's never been taught
You feel his pain, but do nothing, saying the situation he's in, is not your fault
Although there are no visible tears, you know his heart cries
His quest for love, you can see in his eyes
You could make the difference; you could be a blessing in disguise
If God can sacrifice his only begotten son from above
Why can't you take a little of your time, and give back some real love?
Sometimes you have to reach out, even to a complete stranger
You never know who you could be entertaining
It could be one of God's Heavenly Angels
Whoever imagined the Son of God wrapped in swaddling clothes and lying in a manger?

Who Is To Blame?

Little innocent children having fun
Calling themselves, the best of friends
Playing with a loaded gun
Not knowing, a life was about the end!

Playing police and robbers, and pointing the gun
Thinking it was just another toy
Then from him, his little friend would run
He was only a child, a little boy!

Too young to know life's true meaning
Just laughing and playing in the street
Laying in a casket now, as if he's dreaming
Our maker, he has gone to meet!

His little friend, puzzled, not understanding what's wrong
Everybody's crying and shaking their head
Not realizing his playmate is forever gone
Too young to understand, his friend is dead!

So we ask, "Who is at fault?
To whom did the gun belong?"
Maybe a valuable lesson was taught
A little innocent child, will never return home!

A Little Child Shall Lead Them

Eyes have not seen and ears have not heard
Living peacefully together, predators and their prey
No need to feel inferior or scared
And a little child shall lead the way!

Over the flock, a little child will be the shepherd
A kid will lay down with the leopard
A wolf and a lamb shall play together each day
And a little child shall lead the way!

When God rules this world and brings about peace
Oh! What a glorious day!
When we all come together and meet
And a little child shall lead the way!

Never Underestimate Your Child

Stop referring to your child as a mistake
Because after a one night stand, the daddy went away
To a child, that's one of the worse things you can say
You knew the man was not ready for fatherhood on the first date
When he wanted premarital sex, you asked him to wait
But when he made the move you did not hesitate
Then a couple of months later, you thought you were just late
You found out you were pregnant, and this you did not anticipate
So don't take it out on the child because you did not wait
In your child's life, you need to participate
So there will be one parent, with whom he can relate
You will see amazing results once you start to educate
A child's capacity, you can never underestimate
He could grow up to be the next President of the United States
And if you were there by his side, wouldn't that be great?
For being his biggest supporter and motivator, it's you, they would
Congratulate!

Short
Story
Poetry

Standing At The Altar

I remember all the long talks we use to have
You would say, "Lord give me a God fearing country gal
Nothing to glamorous or nothing to dull, maybe something in
between."
Followed by, "Lord, you know what I mean."
I remember the day I blessed you, and answered your prayer
You were so nervous and speechless, but I was standing right there
I put the words in your mouth that you needed to say
You were so mesmerized by her beauty, that it took your breath
away
I remember so clearly the first date the two of you went on
I anxiously awaited to hear about it from you, when you arrived
home
We talked and talked, sometimes for hours at time
You would go to bed and wake up with her on your mind
The days quickly became months, and before you knew it, some
years had passed
You came to me; there was a question you needed to ask
You wanted to ask her for her hand in marriage,
But wanted to know if the time was right
You asked me to give you a sign, as you laid in bed that night
Again, like a loving Father, I did as you asked
Giving you what your heart desired, a wife at last
As you begin to make arrangements for your wedding date
You continually praised me, for giving you a helpmate
Not once did you go to bed without talking to me, we were the best
of friends
Whatever decision you had to make, you always included me in
That was, up until the night of your wedding, when you repeated
your vows
This would be the last time you would call my name out for a while
For some time you had everything going your way
But then you stopped talking to me, you felt you had no need to
pray
Your burdens that I made so light, you now carried

That's why the storms began to brew in your marriage
I gave you all that you needed, as well as the desires of your heart
But then you left me out, that's why things fell apart
You invited me to the wedding, but you didn't take me to your new home
My dear child, that is where you went wrong
I will never leave or forsake you; in your heart is where I always want to be
Standing at the altar, is where you chose to leave me!

A Lost Society

I don't know about you, but it hurts me to my heart
To see how far families have grown apart
Mothers against daughters, and fathers against sons
No longer able to sit at the dinner table together and have fun
A lost society, whose way of solving problems is with a gun!
To your unborn babies bringing harm
Never allowing them a chance to be born
Disposing of them if they do make it here
How can you hurt something so precious and dear?
 And not feel any kind of remorse or fear?
A lost society, God's voice you cannot hear!
On drugs, all strung out
Having no earthly idea what life is all about
Even little innocent children are being used
To sell and distribute drugs throughout the local schools
To support your habit, your parents, you will abuse
A lost society, whose minds are totally confused!
Using God's name to gain children's trust
Only to get close to them, because it's their bodies you lust
A lost society, that feels to get what you want; lying is a must!
A little child's innocence you will betray
In order to get things to go your way
A lost society, that don't believe, God will have the last say!
Leaving nice homes to join dangerous gangs
For initiation, to your own body, you will bring tremendous pain
And for no reason at all, taking people out with a bang
A lost society, that's gone totally insane!
Walking around with your pants sagging to the ground
As if you pulled them out of a box of lost and found
Sometimes looking like a boy, and sometimes looking like a girl
As if you didn't know what you was born to be when brought into
this world
Two or three holes in your ears with the big rings
Holes in your belly button, nose and tongue, holes in anything

A lost society, that even when the name Jesus is spoken, nothing it means!
Whatever you feel you want from others you just go out and take
Because of your laziness, your own money you won't make
Living like a fugitive, moving from place to place
Never learning from any of your mistakes
A lost society, whose hearts are full of a lot of hate!
Going from person to person having sex, and not worried about protection
And for that person, not having any feelings of love, no affection
A lost society, that refuses to show God's reflection!

When You've Done It To The Least Of Them

As I approached a stop sign one day at the end of the street
I observed a sign that read; homeless, will work for money or food
to eat
Negative thoughts crossed my mind right away
What if this individual was a fraud, would I be his victim today?
I began to look this person over thoroughly, through and through
As I wrestled in my mind with, what was the right thing to do
His clothes were pretty clean, but it looked as though he could use a
pair of shoes
I was bound and determined to find out if this man really
Needed my help; I wasn't going to be used
I proceeded to let my window down, surely if he was homeless
He would have a bad smell
But to my surprise, a sweet fragrance filled the air;
He smelled very well
My next thought was to ask him a question; I felt if he was
Homeless, he couldn't be very bright
But before I could speak, he asked, "Ms., Are you alright?"
I immediately let my window up and drove away
He couldn't possibly be homeless I thought, I refused to be a victim
this day
On my way to church the following Sunday, I wondered should
I warn the members, should I share my interesting story
To my surprise, during altar call ,I heard a deep voice from the
Back, shout, "Give Him Glory!"
It was the man from the street corner with the sign
I didn't know what to think at this time
He began to tell how he was once a college professor and living very well
But he was struck with an illness, lost everything,
But now he had an even better story to tell
He testified how he fell to his knees and began to seek God and pray
How he had moved from shelter to shelter, and never went hungry
one day
He told of strangers opening their doors to feed him
And giving him clothes that were new

He witnessed that while you're in the storm, God is there to guide you through
On this day, one family put him in a home rent-free

He continued to praise God, giving Him the victory
At that very moment, I was convicted by the Holy Spirit
I was so busy judging the man, that when God spoke, I didn't hear it
As tears flowed down my face, the preacher asked, "How many of you would have
By passed this young man if you seen him with his sign on the street?
What if you knew it was Jesus, would you have given him shelter and food to eat?
When you turn away one of God's children, do you not understand,
With your spiritual eyes, do you not see?
When you have done it unto one of these my brethren, God said, "Ye have done it unto me!"

Being Grateful: A Christmas Story

Many people will awake running to see what's under the Christmas
tree
This blessed Christmas morn
Never knowing its true significance, the day Christ was born
Some will be sad and disappointed as they look under the
Christmas tree
Finding no presents, asking, "Did Santa forget about me?"
Some will be furious because they purchased an expensive gift from
the mall
Only to receive a gift purchased from the Dollar Store,
In their eyesight, worth nothing at all
Some will be overwhelmed because everything they asked for,
They found under the tree
But again, some will ask tearfully, "Did Santa forget about me?"
Travel with me to grandma's house as she tries to cheer up her little
grandson
As the meaning of being grateful is truly learned
"Grandma," little Jimmy asked, "Why aren't there any presents
under the tree?
"Is it because nobody cares, or loves me?"
"Oh, my little Angel," she replied,
"You know you are the apple of Grandma's eyes."
There was a loud knock at the door at the this time
It's got to be Santa, Little Jimmy thought over and over in his mind
With his eyes all bucked, expecting a bug surprise
It was a neighbor bringing him a pair of old shoes,
Tears quickly filled his little eyes
"Grandma," again he asked, "Why come no one thought about me?"
"My little Angel," she said, "Come and sit on Grandma's knee."
"Little Jimmy, the kind lady bought you a pair of shoes."
"But Grandma," he said, "I can't play with them, and they are old
and used."
"My child, you had no shoes to wear; remember,
That is why you could not go out to play?"
"That is right grandma," he said, "Now I can go outside today."
Suddenly at the door, there was another knock

Little Jimmy ran excitedly again to answer, but quickly came to a stop
It was another neighbor leaving groceries on the broken down steps
He ran to grandma hiding his face, as he sadly wept
Grandma hugged him tight as she reminded him of the previous night
"Little Jimmy, I watched you in your bed as you tossed and turned
Grandma had nothing in the cabinet; for food, your little body yearned
So be grateful, we now have food to eat."
He then said with a grin, "And don't forget, I also have shoes for my feet."
For the third time there was a knock at the door
Little Jimmy ran to answer it, still expecting more
It was the pastor and some members from the church

Coming to do some house repairs, and much needed yard work
To Grandma's surprise, little Jimmy responded with a smile on his face
He said, "Grandma, you always try to explain to me about God's mercy and grace
Now I think I understand."
He walked closer and took her by the hand
"God sent these men to fix the doors and windows so the air
Can't blow in, because it is so cold
As I coughed in bed, you watched over me and cleaned my sore, runny nose
God did not put our presents under the tree
He loves us so much, He sent them over one by one for us to see!"
This time, Grandma's eyes were filled with tears
As she thanked God for all her blessed Christmas years
There was another knock at the door; "Grandma you get it,"
Little Jimmy happily said
As Grandma looked out, all she could do was shake her head
There stood a big bad of goodies, not only for Little Jimmy, but for her too
There was no one there visibly to thank; so Grandma looked up and said,
"Lord I Thank You!"

The Man Behind The Mask
(A Sinner's Plea)

Pretending to have it all together and doing fine
Knowing I'm living on the edge, about to lose my mind
Feeling like a prisoner bound by chains in my own home
In solitary confinement, separated from the rest, all alone
Striving to do the right thing, but unable to break free
There's a tug of war, a conflict in my mind, I'm in captivity
Living one life by day and another by night
Like a time bomb about to explode, I'm losing the fight
Wanting to tell loved ones of the struggles I face
What will they think of me, will I be a disgrace?
How long can I hide the guilt and scars from the kids?
What will they think of a dad who keeps his real face hid?
A wife wanting so bad to believe her husband's lies
How long can I pretend I don't see the hurt in her eyes?
How can I love something so much,
And destroy it at the same time?
Should I just leave, while she still has a piece of mind?
I'm holding on by a thin thread, barely able to cope
Will I be able to pull off the mask, is there any hope?
Have I fallen so far down that I'm out of God's reach
Am I the devil's advocate for keeps?
When I think of what I use to be and what I have become
The pressure begins to build, and back to my old comfort zone I run
Drinking and shooting up with old familiar faces
Hanging out all night in run down ungodly places
Struggling to move forward, but I keep going back to my past
How long can I pretend, will I ever be able to remove the mask?
I have become handicapped by my addictions and I know I need
help
So Lord I come to you in confidence, because my secret you have so
honestly kept
I don't really know you, but I'm at a point that I'm willing to give you
a try

I've heard my wife talk to you for sometime in the midnight hour as she cry
So with a sincere heart and on both knees I ask,
Can you come into my life and help me take off the mask?

The Missionary That Use To Be On A Mission

One Saturday evening, Grandma Lilly, known as Nanna,
Sat outside in her favorite swing
As she talked with her granddaughter Sarah, who was at a very curious age,
And asked all sorts of things
She asked, "Nanna, why do you call yourself a missionary,
And what do you mean by doing good deeds?"
Nanna responded, "Well, I used to go around sharing the good news of Jesus Christ with others, and helping those that were in need."
"Why did you stop Grandma, when there are still so many mouths to feed?"
 Nanna said, "I'm old and feeble now, these old legs can't walk as far, they get tired and hurt."
Sarah responded quickly,
"You don't have to walk far, you can help with the food ministry at the church."
With a confused look, little Sarah went on to say, "Nanna you told me that a missionary never sits down on God, there's always something you can do.
What's wrong Nanna, did you tell me something that was untrue?"
"No Sarah, I would never lie to you", she said
As she thought silently, "To Christ, I have become dead?
I use to be on fire for the Lord, where did I go wrong?
How could I sit down on God, and do nothing for so long?
There are devoted church members who can't come to church anymore due to their health
Who am I to complain, how can I be so focused only on myself?
Children and seniors are still being misused and abused
I can't get comfortable now; By God, I can still be used
What kind of example am I setting?
What if God sat down on me?
Oh Lord, she cried out,
Forgive me for not being all that I could be."

Breaking her train of thought, Sarah yelled, "Nanna, did you hear me?"

As if she had gone deaf

"Yes Sarah, I hear you loud and clear, and I'll serve him with all that I have left!"

Learning How To Humble Yourself And Trust God

Oh Lord, I was in such a hurry today
 I did not have time to kneel and pray
Got to work only to find out that my job was no longer there
They had to downsize due to the economy,
I am sure that you are already aware
You know, lately God, I have really been going through
I have been praying for a while now, nothings changed,
I don't know what else to do
Lord all of my bills are past due and I don't have a dime
My best friend said I should apply for government assistance;
But Lord you know I'm not standing in no welfare line
I even spoke with the pastor and he asked me to come down to the altar so he could pray
I declined; I did not want people looking at me strange;
Besides, behind my back, what would they say?
You know that I hold a top-notch position in the church,
And I have to be strong
I did not want people all up in my business, asking me what is wrong
And then to top it off, after service I was approached by Sister Sally Sue
Offering to help me out, saying she was lead by you
Lord, I know you said you would make our enemy our footstool, but I am no fool
I know people like that, you don't use
You know she started all that mess in the church two years ago
So I told her a piece of my mind, she was not lead by your spirit, I know
By the way Lord, I shorted you on my tithes today at church
Just in case you blessed me with a job this week,
I'll need it for gas to make it to work
If nobody else understands Lord, my best friend says you do
So I should just go home and rest, and wait on you
It's been two weeks Lord, and I seem to be in even worse shape

My best friend would not steer me wrong, so I guess I'll sit and wait
You know my husband was not acting right, so she suggested
That I get rid of him too; I am all alone now, I'm just in a fix
She said that he was no good, and would never change,
Cause you can't teach something old, new tricks
Come to think of it, You know I have not seen my best friend in a
couple of weeks
But the other day sister Sally Sue came strutting up the street
As she knocked on my door, again, saying she had something to
share with me,
And was being led by your spirit
I let her in, feeling this time, I had to hear it
I tried everything else, and all had failed
I was tired and weary; about to give up, I was living in hell
As we read the scriptures, we began to pray
Lord you came like a mighty wind, in such a powerful way
I had to lose all of my worldly possessions
To gain You truly in the end
I now have joy that the world can't take away, and a new best friend!

Dedications

Remembering The Good Old Days

As a child, I can remember traveling down the old Kilgore Highway
Going to see big momma and big deddy,
Not knowing how long daddy would leave me to stay
As long as I had my cousins to play with, I was okay
My grandparents were never to busy for us
If we called big deddy, he came right on.
Never once, did I hear him fuss
He would drive through the Tyler streets in his old green truck
making his rounds
We would jump on the back, and if we seen a familiar face, we would
duck our heads down
Shouting out and having fun as we strolled through town
Upon our arrival, my big mama would always come out and greet us
with a smile
Stuffing us with her sweet potato pies, making our stay worth the
while
I remember when we as children played outside all day
We were not allowed around grown folks, listening and repeating
what they had to say
I remember making mud pies and climbing trees, the good old
fashion kind of fun
We did not know anything about video games, or playing with
loaded guns
If we wanted to play paper dolls, we simply cut them out of a catalog
book
We knew nothing of the Ken and Barbie fashion look
I remember playing cowboys and Indians with an old mop and
broom
That was what we called having fun; not staying secluded all day in
our room
It was of no importance what brand name of clothing we would wear
We did not spend all day in the beauty shop, it was press or
naturally wash and wear
We were not given too many chances back in the day if we done
something wrong

It was not boy or girl, just wait till you get home
There was no court system telling our parents what to do
Wherever you showed out, that's where they would get you
We were taught to respect anyone that was grown
They had a right to discipline you, and you would get punished
when you got home
I say to my parents and grandparents, thanks for instilling in me
The true and real meaning of a family!

Dedicated in memory of my Grandparents; Stafford and Clara
Warren

Keeping The Faith

Have you ever read in the Bible, The Book of Job?
How God allowed the devil to tempt him, but not touch his soul?
Remember how Job suffered, but to the devil, he did not give in?
He stood on God's promise until the very end.
His own wife tried to discourage him, but he still kept the faith,
He did not give the devil victory, on God, he did wait.
He was not only sick for so long, but everything he had he lost,
But still he did not allow Satan to be his boss.
He truly withstood the tests of faith for the Lord,
Losing everything you have, has got to be pretty hard.
Sometimes I feel like God is taking us through a test,
We start out doing pretty good, and then we give less, and less.
We start to get tired because the night seems so long,
But we have to keep on fighting, until God say, "It is time to come home."
We do not like to suffer or feel any kind of pain,
But God said if you suffer with Him, you would also reign!
He never promised that there would be sunshine everyday,
But every once in a while, the rain would come our way.
We have to lean and depend on God, and stop putting our trust in man,
Because no one has the power to do what God can!
If you go to the doctor and he says you are sick, and there is no cure,
You are sometimes quick to forget,
God is a healing doctor, and He is always standing near.
Waiting for you to call on Him, because your pain He can feel,
But you must know beyond the shadow of a doubt, your sickness,
God can heal.
Although it seems that each day is a challenge,
Sometimes to just get up out of your bed,
Pick up your Bible, and read the Book of Job, and then meditate on
what you read,
It is here you will get your inspiration, because your soul will be fed!

Dedicated to Ms. Gloria Moore, a good friend that is determined to
beat cancer!

No Limit To What God Can Do

Can you recall the bad accident you were in, and everyone had given up in you?
God healed your broken bones and brought you through
There is no limit to what God can do!
After the stroke, the doctors said you would never walk again
Then you prayed, and allowed Jesus to come in
You can now run, jump, shout, and bend
There is no limit to what God can do, when you open the door and let Him in!
Do you remember after the heart attack
You were lying flat on your back and could not move?
The doctors said your heart was no longer any good,
And all of your vital signs you would quickly lose
But God stepped in, and your heart muscles, He began to soothe
You rose up off of your sick bed, leaving the doctors totally confused
You can't put a limit on what can happen, when God is being used!
Remember when your sugar level went up,
You went into a coma and could not respond?
The doctors done all that they could do, they were all stunned
Then it was like God touched you with a magic wand!
Do you remember when you got sick
And the doctors put you in the hospital to run tests?
They were steady poking you with needles, and you could not get any rest
They had no clue as to what was wrong, but that, they would never confess
Your body was so tired and weak, but you refused to become depressed
As you lay helplessly, you asked for Doctor Jesus, the very best
He miraculously healed your body;
There is no limit to what God can do, so don't settle for less
There are a lot of walking and talking miracles on this earth right today
God came through, when man said there was no way
So when obstacles come up against you and you're scared

Try him for yourself; don't just take someone's word
Make it a personal thing, not something you heard
Remember, through God, you can conquer all things
There is no limit to the number of blessings in your life, that He can
bring!

Dedicated to Sandra Long

Finding Joy In The Midst of Your Storm

The devil knows that you are God's child, so in your life he will be persistent
Doing whatever he can to bring you down; but to his will, you must remain resistant
Remember, God holds all power in his hand, he spoke the whole world into existence
The devil's job is to kill, steal, and destroy
But knowing God in the midst of your storm, you can still find joy!
People won't understand why on your face there's still a smile
When they know you are going through such difficult trials
Through the tears, suffering, and sometimes constant pain
It is a closer relationship with our Heavenly Father you have gained
So while in the midst of your storm
Find joy in knowing that God is carrying you safely in His Heavenly arms!
And as long as he gives you strength, continue to run the race
Find joy in knowing, one day you shall see his face
And upon your head, God shall place a crown,
And on your back, a pair of angelic wings
For running the race with faith, no matter how hard it seemed!

Dedicated to Mrs. Mable Mumphrey on 10/30/02
Sunrise: November 22, 1953 - Sunset: February 12, 2003

62

No Charge

For the fifteen years I have spent with you
Playing for you and teaching you
No charge!
For the time I have spent learning how to play the songs you wanted
to sing
For the money I have spent to get the music, I never asked you for
one thing
There was no charge!
For all of the extra rehearsals for special engagements
Never, did I ask you for one cent
There was no charge!
For all the trips, there was a cost for my gas
Not for so much, as for one penny, did I ever ask
There was no charge!
For the wear and tear on my car over the years
For all the times the choir didn't act right, and I felt like shedding
tears
Again, there was no charge!
For all the times my body was so worn out and tired
I persevered on, knowing everything I needed, the Lord would
provide
For you, there was no charge!
For all God has blessed me with, nothing in this world could ever
measure up to
That is why I have played for fifteen years, at no charge to you
So when you add my bill up, you will see, the total cost for my
Love is
NO CHARGE!

Dedicated to Ms. Mijoi Bowens

God's Helper

One who truly gives of themselves
Putting their own agenda behind everyone else
Loving, sharing, and caring for those in need
Always willing to do a good deed
No matter how big or small the situation
Always stepping out on faith, without hesitation
Not waiting on others to say what they will do
Like troops on the battlefield, doing what you have to
Standing boldly like God's helper should be
Thank you Cathy Burton for being the light
That shines for all the world to see!

Dedicated to Cathy Burton

God's Beautiful Butterfly

The last thing I remember was falling into this deep sleep
But when I awoke, I was different form my head to my feet
I started to stretch my arms, but instead I had wings
I am the most beautiful and elegant thing
Like a rainbow, I have such an array of colors
There is so much I have yet to discover
I feel bound by nothing, I feel so free
As the wind blows beneath my wings, it lifts me
I am now flying high in God's beautiful butterfly garden above
I feel no hurt, no discomfort, nothing but love
Everything here is divine, and I am at peace
So let your tears be tears of joy, not of grief
And if one day, a butterfly should land on your shoulder and
You think of me, know that I too, miss you very much
So don't jump or flinch my love ones, just think of it as me
Keeping in touch!

Dedicated to Marty Lancione
In Loving Memory of His Wife
Sherry Lancione
Sunrise: October 18, 1961 – Sunset: September 19, 2005

The Angels In Heaven Are Rejoicing

There are many who said you would give up and not make it this far
But with your faith and God's grace, look at where you are
There were even some who wanted you to fail
But now that you have made it, you have a testimony to tell
For those non-believers who quit, or won't even try
You have to tell them to persevere on, and the reason why
God did not deliver you to keep it to yourself
There are some who feel like it can't be done and need to hear
It from someone like yourself
The devil is angry now, and he will try even harder to put
Stumbling blocks in your way
So don't get discouraged, just never stop ceasing to pray
When one door closes, God opens another; he will be there for you
He will continue to give you strength to climb your mountains,
And see you through
Continue to read God's word, and believe it, because it won't return
void
If God said it, it shall come to pass, for Him, nothing is too hard
Always remember, there is a silver lining behind every dark cloud
Keep on keeping on my sister, just wanted to let you know
I'm very proud!

Dedicated to Anita Hagen

You Can't Fool God

You can never fool God, so why even try?
He knows beforehand, who what, when, where and why
Didn't you know, He has an all seeing eye?
So before you put all your time and energy into doing wrong
Remember, God is still sitting high,
Watching from his throne
He has a memory that will never fade away
As he records how you live from day to day
So if you are one that thinks you have God fooled
You are greatly mistaken; This is one bet, you lose!

Acknowledgements

First and foremost, I thank God for His guidance. I would like to thank my husband, Lonnie Johnson, for always encouraging me to share with the world, what God shared with me. When you're blessed with a spouse that loves the Lord like you, and stands by your side through the good and bad, you have to give God the praise. A special thanks to my parents, Marcellus and Betty Warren for always believing in me. To Salisa Caldwell, a very dear friend that God has put before me in certain seasons in my life, I am so grateful. For all of my family members and friends, words cannot express the love and appreciation I feel in my heart for you. To all of the believers and unbelievers, I thank you for being a part in my spiritual growth. If I had not gone through the tests, I would not have a testimony.

Proofreader's Profile

Reverend Orenthia Mason
Current pastor of Cole Hill Christian Methodist Episcopal
Church. She is a 1970 honor graduate of Emmett J. Scott, and a
1973 graduate of Texas College, leading her class with the honors
of Magna Cum Laude. She has held many positions in the Tyler
Independent School District. She currently serves as the Director
of Teacher Education, at Jarvis Christian College.

Mrs. Patricia Cross
A 1972 graduate of Chapel Hill High School. She is also a 1974
graduate of Tyler Junior College, where she obtained an Associate of
Art Degree. Mrs. Cross resides in Winona, Texas with her husband,
Billy Cross, of 27 years. She currently serves as an Educational Aide
for Winona Independent School District. She is an active member
of the Christian Methodist Episcopal Church. She enjoys her
gift of music by playing the piano. She likes reading, writing, and
organizing.

Mrs. Lelia Scott Bowens- Henry
Graduate of Jackson High School and Chapel Hill Independent
School District. She attended the University of Texas at Tyler
Master of Education, and Tyler Real Estate College. She is currently
a retired school teacher of 35 years. Mrs. Henry is an active member
and musician at Cole Hill Christian Methodist Episcopal Church.

About the Author

The Author was born, Jacqueline Evon Warren, to Marcellus and Betty Warren of Tyler, Texas. She currently resides in Tyler, with her husband, Lonnie Johnson. They are the proud parents of Breanna and Christopher Johnson. She is a 1982 graduate of John Tyler High School, and a 15 year associate at Tyler's north side Walmart. She is an active member of the Cole Hill Christian Methodist Episcopal Church, currently under the leadership of Reverend Orenthia Mason. She enjoys writing and working with children.

CPSIA information can be obtained at www.ICGtesting.com
Printed in the USA
LVOW121744280812

296357LV00004B/27/A